NOVELLO
classics
for the flute

W.A. Mozart

Flute Concerto No.2 in D
K.314

Andante in C
K.315

Edited by
Trevor Wye
Piano arrangement by
Robert Scott

Novello Publishing Limited

Order No. NOV 120578

Cover design and typesetting by Malcolm Harvey Young.

French translation by Agnès Ausseur.
German translation by Gunhild Lenz-Mulligan.
Italian translation by Luigi Suvini.

Contents

Concerto No.2 in D K.314

The two flute concertos, K.313 and K.314, and the Andante in C, K.315, were written in Mannheim in 1778 to fulfil a commission from a Dutch physician and amateur flute player, Ferdinand Dejean (1731–1797). This commission, arranged by the Mannheim Court flautist, Wendling, (Johann Baptist Wendling, 1723–1797), was for 'three short, simple concertos and a couple of quartets for the flute' for a fee of 200 gulden. After writing the first concerto, Mozart found that time was running out, so in order to complete the commission he transcribed his earlier Oboe Concerto in C into D major to make the second flute concerto.

Of the two concertos, the only surviving autographs are of the Andante in C and the solo oboe part of the Oboe Concerto, though there is doubt about the authenticity of the latter. It is likely that the Andante in C was written as an easier alternative to the second movement of the D major Concerto.

It is recorded that, after his death, the effects of a certain amateur flute player, Dejean, were auctioned. Among the items was a trunk containing 'music manuscripts'...

Period instruments The exact type of flute used by Wendling and Dejean to perform Mozart's music is not known, but assumed to be the one-keyed flute common at that time, with four joints and an internal diameter of between 18.6 and 19mm. For the Flute and Harp Concerto in C, however, the Duc de Guines (a former ambassador to London), must surely have used the six-keyed English flute, with its foot joint extension down to low C.

Mozart's 'dislike' of the flute In a letter to his father on 14th February 1778, Mozart wrote about the flute: 'whenever I have to write music for an instrument I dislike, I immediately lose interest'. Mozart's remark, however, was probably coloured by the fact that Dejean had failed to pay him fully for the concertos and quartets he had commissioned; it is also possible that Mozart had less enthusiasm for writing for an amateur player. The flute, with its cross-fingered notes, gained a reputation for being played out of tune and this too, may have affected his comments.

Mozart's remark has been widely quoted and exaggerated, although he wrote some wonderful solos for the flute. His later orchestral works show no signs of dislike for the instrument he reputedly loved to hate. In addition, Mozart is reported to have made the following observation about the flautist Wendling: '...you don't always have to be afraid with him when you know a note is about to come out that it is going to be much too low or too high... his heart is in the right place and so are his ears and the tip of his tongue...'

Concerto No.2 en ré K.314

Les deux concertos pour flûte, K.313 et K.314, et l'*Andante* en *ut*, K.315, furent composés par Mozart à Mannheim en 1778, à la demande d'un médecin et flûtiste amateur, Ferdinand Dejean (1731–1797). Cette commande de "trois concertos courts et simples et de quelques quatuors pour la flûte" fut passée à l'instigation du flûtiste de la cour de Mannheim, Johann Baptist Wendling (1723–1797) pour un cachet de 200 gulden. Après avoir écrit le premier concerto, Mozart ne disposait plus d'assez de temps. Il transposa donc son Concerto pour hautbois d'*ut* majeur en *ré* majeur pour en faire le deuxième concerto pour flûte et honorer la commande.

Les deux seuls manuscrits autographes subsistants des deux concertos sont ceux de l'*Andante* en *ut* et de la partie de soliste du Concerto pour hautbois, quoique demeure un doute sur l'authenticité de ce dernier. Il semblerait que l'*Andante* en *ut* ait été écrit comme alternative plus facile au deuxième mouvement du Concerto en *ré* majeur.

Il a été rapparté que parmi les effets vendus aux enchères, après sa mort, d'un certain Dejean, flûtiste amateur, se trouvait une malle contenant des "manuscrits de musique"...

Instruments anciens On ne connaît pas le type exact de flûte utilisée par Wendling et Dejean pour jouer la musique de Mozart mais on pense qu'il s'agit de la flûte à une clef, à quatre corps et d'un diamètre interne de 18,6 à 19mm, courante à cette époque. Toutefois, pour le Concerto pour flûte et harpe en *ut*, le duc de Guines (ancien ambassadeur à Londres) a sûrement joué une flûte anglaise à six clefs dont le corps inférieur supplémentaire étend le registre au *do* grave.

L'"aversion" de Mozart pour la flûte Dans une lettre à son père datée du 14 février 1778, Mozart écrivit au sujet de la flûte: "A chaque fois que je dois écrire de la musique pour un instrument que je n'aime pas, je me désintéresse immédiatement." Cette remarque de Mozart, toutefois, était sans doute teintée par le fait que Dejean ne lui avait pas totalement réglé les concertos et les quatuors qu'il lui avait commandés. Il se peut aussi que Mozart ait montré moins d'enthousiasme à écrire pour un amateur. De plus, la flûte, avec ses doigtés croisés, avait la réputation d'être fausse, ce qui a pu influencer ces commentaires.

Cette réflexion de Mozart a été largement citée et surfaite bien qu'il ait composé de merveilleux solos de flûte. Ses dernières oeuvres orchestrales ne présentent pas le moindre signe d'éloignement pour l'instrument qu'il aurait tant détesté. Mozart aurait également dit en parlant du flûtiste Wendling: "...Il n'y a pas de souci à se faire avec lui quand on sait qu'un note va venir et qu'on s'attend à ce qu'elle soit ou trop basse ou trop haute... Son coeur est à la bonne place, ainsi que ses oreilles et le bout de sa langue..."

Editorial Policy

Unless otherwise indicated, the earliest known sources have been adhered to and the flute part can be considered 'urtext'. Suggested nuances have been placed in brackets and slurs which may well have been used in Mozart's time are shown by dotted lines. Performers on the modern flute may care to omit the slurs with lines through them to achieve longer line phrases. Tuttis have been omitted though the performer may play them if desired.

The piano part in modern editions is usually a reduction of the orchestral score and as a result is often cluttered by unnecessary material which renders it unplayable by all but the most advanced pianists. As these concertos are most often performed with the piano, we have approached the problem of the orchestral reduction as Mozart might have done – by writing for the piano in its own right and not as a substitute for the orchestra. The piano arrangement is modelled on Mozart's violin and piano sonata writing. As a result, superfluous material has been omitted, though the original notation and the bowing of the string parts has been carefully adhered to.

Performing Notes

Performing Style As Franz Vester has pointed out, these works were written in a period when the late baroque style was in vogue... 'this is dancing and talking music – not singing music'. Articulation is the language of music and therefore clarity (together with the use of the slur) is of particular importance to these concertos. In eighteenth century music, a slur should also be viewed as a *diminuendo...* except sometimes! So the slur and all it implies governs the phrasing to a large degree.

There is a close connection between the solo part and the accompaniment and study of the piano score is important in order to observe the way in which the character of the orchestral writing can influence the performance of the solo part. On a modern Boehm flute, the performer has several options depending upon the occasion of the performance: as has already been suggested, the modern player could leave out the slurs with lines through them to achieve longer 'lines' and phrases. Competitors, on the other hand, might play everything which is urtext to avoid negative criticism, (or they may be wise to play in a style the judges wish to hear, though a freshness of approach can score points). For a recording, the performer has to come to terms with the fact that their interpretation of this evergreen will be forever frozen on disc... Flautists of this century have generally adopted a romantic style with 'long line' phrases; it is also common to hear long (conceivably overlong) cadenzas.

Principes d'édition

A moins d'une indication contraire, cette édition se fonde sur les premières sources connues et l'on peut considérer la partie de flûte comme *'Urtext'*. Les nuances et liaisons suggérées, qui ont pu être exécutées du temps de Mozart, sont indiquées en pointillé ou placées entre parenthèses. On pourra, sur une flûte moderne, éviter les liaisons barrées pour obtenir un tracé de phrase plus long. Les Tuttis ont été supprimés mais l'interprète peut les jouer s'il le désire.

La partie de piano des éditions modernes est en général une réduction de la partition d'orchestre, souvent inutilement encombrée et, de ce fait, exclusivement accessible à des pianistes très avancés. Ces concertos étant le plus souvent exécutés avec le piano, nous avons abordé la question de la réduction d'orchestre comme Mozart lui-même l'aurait fait – en écrivant pour le piano en tant que tel et non comme substitut de l'orchestre. L'arrangement pour piano s'inspire du modèle d'écriture des sonates pour violon et piano de Mozart. Les éléments superflus en ont été écartés tout en maintenant scrupuleusement la notation originale et les coups d'archet des cordes.

Notes sur l'exécution

Le style de jeu Ainsi que Franz Vester l'a relevé, ces oeuvres datent d'une époque où le style baroque tardif était en faveur... "C'est de la musique qui danse et qui parle – pas de la musique qui chante." Le phrasé en structure le discours et la clarté (procédant du recours aux liaisons) est d'une importance particulière dans ces concertos. Dans la musique du dix-huitième siècle, une liaison pouvait également signifier un *diminuendo...*mais pas toujours! La liaison et tout ce qu'elle implique régissent donc le phrasé dans une large proportion.

Le lien entre la partie de soliste et l'accompagnement est étroit et l'analyse de la partition de piano est essentielle afin d'observer la manière dont l'écriture orchestrale peut influencer l'exécution de la partie de soliste. Sur une flûte Boehm moderne, l'interprète a le choix entre plusieurs options en fonction des circonstances de son exécution. Comme on l'a déjà mentionné, il peut laisser de côté les liaisons barrées de manière à définir des 'lignes' et des phrases plus longues. Les candidats à un examen, en revanche, joueront de préférence tous les éléments de l'*Urtext* pour éviter les critiques négatives (ou adopteront le style que le jury souhaite entendre, bien qu'une certaine fraîcheur d'approche puisse marquer des points). Lors d'un enregistrement, l'exécutant se soumettra aux implications de la gravure définitive de son interprétation de cette oeuvre éternelle sur le disque... Les flûtistes actuels s'attachent généralement à un style romantique aux phrases longues dont les cadences étendues (voire très étendues) ne sont pas rares.

Ornaments

CPE Bach wrote that nobody ever doubted that ornaments were necessary. Ornaments serve to link notes together, to enliven a particular note or phrase, and to draw the listener's attention to them. Mozart wrote these concertos during a change in ornamental style, so it is particularly difficult for us to know exactly how the ornaments are to be played. In this edition, performers can see for themselves the earliest written sources and make a judgement accordingly. Those with little specialist knowledge may care to follow the editorial suggestions (either placed in brackets or above the stave) which are based on present day informed opinion[1]. The two ornaments which will concern us are *appoggiaturas* and *trills*.

Appoggiaturas: accented appoggiaturas usually appear as a small note whose written value does not always indicate the rhythm to be played. The suggested rhythm has been shown above the stave on its first appearance; the player should follow this in subsequent examples. But why didn't Mozart simply write the rhythm he wanted to be played? Appoggiaturas[2] indicate a special stress or a dissonance, or sometimes they draw the listener's attention to the note to which the appoggiatura is attached. It is a useful device and marks a distinct indication to the performer. How the appoggiatura is played is more important than its exact value. It *always* steals the emphasis from the note to which it is attached, which follows more softly. The appoggiatura is invariably slurred to its principal note... and a slur is a *diminuendo*.

(First Movement)

Compound appoggiaturas should be played caressingly but quickly:
(Second movement, bars 19, 21, etc.)

(Third movement bar 4)

should be played
devrait être joué

or:
ou:

Bars 60 and 61 in the *Concerto for Oboe* has an alternative scale passage. Performers could use this or substitute their own in quavers (eighth notes), triplet quavers, or in semiquavers (sixteenth notes) to good effect. A comparison with the Oboe Concerto is recommended.

Trills all begin on the upper note...except sometimes! The exceptions are shown either by the omission of an auxiliary note, or by the inclusion of the lower auxiliary. Upper or lower, both

Les ornements

CPE Bach écrivit que personne ne mit jamais en doute la nécessité des ornements. Ils servent à relier les notes, à animer une note ou une phrase spécifiques et à attirer l'attention de l'auditeur sur elles. Mozart composa ces concertos pendant une période de mutation du style ornemental. Il s'avère donc particulièrement difficile de savoir comment jouer exactement les ornements. Les interprètes peuvent ici se reporter aux premières sources écrites et se faire un jugement en conséquence. Ceux dont les connaissances spécialisées sont limitées pourront suivre les suggestions apportées à l'édition (placées soit entre parenthèses, soit au-dessus de la portée) qui reposent sur l'opinion actuelle des spécialistes[1]. Les deux ornements sur lesquels nous insisterons sont les *appogiatures* et les *trilles*.

Les appogiatures accentuées figurent habituellement sous forme d'une petite note dont la valeur n'indique pas nécessairement le rythme à exécuter. Le rythme conseillé est noté au-dessus de la portée lors de sa première apparition et sera reproduit lors de ses occurrences suivantes. Mais pourquoi Mozart n'écrivit-il pas simplement le rythme qu'il voulait voir jouer? L'appogiature[2] marque un appui spécial ou une dissonance et parfois retient l'attention de l'auditeur sur la note à laquelle elle est reliée. C'est un procédé utile qui fournit une indication spécifique à l'interprète. La façon de jouer l'appogiature est plus importante que sa valeur exacte. Elle détourne *toujours* l'importance de la note qu'elle accompagne et qui la suit doucement. L'appogiature est obligatoirement liée à la note réelle...et une liaison signifie un *diminuendo*.

(Premier mouvement)

Les appogiatures composées doivent être exécutées doucement mais rapidement:
(Deuxième mouvement, mesures 19, 21, etc.)

(Troisième mouvement, mesure 4)

Les mesures 60 et 61 du Concerto pour hautbois contiennent un trait de gamme *ad libitum*. Les exécutants peuvent le jouer ou y substituer leur propre passage en croches, triolets de croches ou doubles croches qui tous produiront un bel effet. La confrontation avec le Concerto pour hautbois est recommandée ici.

Tous **les trilles** commencent par la note supérieure... sauf dans certains cas! Les exceptions se reconnaissent soit à l'omission de la note

played *on* the beat. The trill begins on the lower auxiliary when it is approached from below, after a scale passage, or to give more finality at the end of a long section. Suggestions as to which approach are given in this edition. When the trill is a short one, particularly in the faster movements, it is unimportant whether it starts on the upper or principal note.

Mozart is quite clear about whether a turn should or should not be played at the end of a trill. Where nothing is written, none should be played. A turn has the effect of giving finality to the trill as in a cadence; in many cases, however, the trill is simply decorative and is not intended to indicate the end of a section.

(Andante in C, bar 2) for the trill:

too many notes would be out of character. Try:

or:

Cadenzas

A cadenza generally appears towards the end of the movement and is an opportunity to surprise and delight the audience and to encourage applause. The pause on the six-four chord is suspended and interrupted with scales and arpeggios until the appearance of the dominant seventh, leading to its resolution. Contrary to popular belief, these cadenzas would have been relatively short, as a flute player can only play one note at a time so would have to break the harmony and melody to take a breath. So cadenzas were kept to within one or two breaths to maintain the forward motion of the harmony. For an important competition on the other hand, the competitor would be wise to play the kind of cadenza the jury are accustomed to hear...

A few points to bear in mind:
• In a short cadenza, it is not essential to quote from the thematic material.
• Always try to sound spontaneous.
• A cadenza should contain a surprise or two.
• There should be a high point in the cadenza: sometimes it is the highest note or the fastest passage, or even the surprise.
• If there is a cadential trill, then the orchestra, harpsichordist or pianist should play the dominant seventh chord half way through the trill to help carry it forward to the resolution. (That chord is indicated in this edition.)

secondaire ou par l'introduction de la note secondaire inférieure. Supérieure ou inférieure, cette note est attaquée *sur* le temps. Le trille commence sur la note inférieure lorsqu'il est approché d'en dessous, après une gamme ou pour parfaire la terminaison d'une section longue. Notre édition donne quelques suggestions sur l'approche à exécuter. Si le trille est bref, notamment dans les mouvements rapides, il est sans importance de le commencer sur la note principale ou sur la note supérieure.

Mozart précise très clairement si le trille doit être conclu par un *gruppetto*. Si rien n'est écrit, il ne faut rien ajouter. Le *gruppetto* a pour effet de terminer le trille comme une cadence. Dans bien des cas, toutefois, le trille n'est que décoratif et n'est pas destiné à marquer la fin d'une section. (*Andante* en *ut*, mesure 2) pour le trille:

trop de notes ne respecteraient pas ici le caractère. Essayez:

ou:

Les cadences

La cadence se place généralement à la fin d'un mouvement et représente l'occasion de surprendre, de ravir et de susciter les applaudissements du public. La pause sur l'accord de quarte et sixte est suspendue et interrompue par des motifs de gammes et d'arpèges conduisant à la septième de dominante et à sa résolution. Contrairement à une opinion courante, les cadences étaient relativement courtes, un flûtiste ne pouvant jouer qu'une note à la fois et devant interrompre l'harmonie et la mélodie pour reprendre son souffle. Les cadences étaient donc contenues à l'intérieur d'une ou deux respirations pour maintenir la progression harmonique. Lors d'une audition importante, le candidat sera avisé d'exécuter le genre de cadence auquel le jury est habitué...

Voici quelques points à garder à l'esprit:
• Dans une cadence courte, il n'est pas essentiel de citer des éléments de la thématique.
• Une cadence doit toujours paraître spontanée.
• Une cadence doit offrir un ou deux coups de théâtre.
• Une cadence doit comporter un sommet: note aiguë, passage rapide ou autre élément inattendu.
• Si la cadence comporte un trille, l'orchestre, le claveciniste ou le pianiste joueront l'accord de septième de dominante au milieu du trille pour aider à le tenir jusqu'à la résolution. (Cet accord est indiqué dans notre édition).

To write your own cadenza using Mozart's material, look through his themes:

(First movement) (Premier mouvement)

(Second movement) (Deuxième mouvement)

and the useful cadence at 38:   et la cadence utile à 38:

(Third movement)
(Troisième mouvement)

*or the oboe version: *ou la version pour hautbois:

(Andante in C)
(*Andante* en *ut*)

Find a short phrase to link the opening pause to the final cadential trill on the dominant seventh chord, For example:
(First movement)

Cherchez un phrase brève qui reliera la pause au trille final de la cadence sur l'accord de septième de dominante. Par exemple:
(Premier mouvement)

A cadenza does not have to start on the given note, nor indeed to end on the printed trill, or even end on a trill at all, in which case, the re-entry into the concerto would constitute a surprise! In

Une cadence ne débute pas nécessairement sur une note donnée, ni ne se termine obligatoirement par le trille imprimé ni aucun autre trille. Le retour au concerto, en l'occurrence, constitue

this example, a trill on C sharp would do just as well as the trill on E:

une surprise! Dans l'exemple suivant, un trille sur *do dièse* serait aussi bon qu'un trille sur *mi:*

This is hardly a cadenza yet but it is a start. To extend your cadenza, use scales and arpeggios – or Mozart's music – to give it some shape. Keep it simple to begin with and only modulate when you are more experienced; even then there should be no more than two modulations in one cadenza. Write your cadenza with barlines: a cadenza doesn't strictly need them but you will be more likely to plan it with the correct phrase lengths and with an overall shape. Finally, be patient: don't expect an immediate and brilliant result – only Mozart could do that!

Here are some easy, short cadenzas as examples:

Ceci constitue à peine une cadence mais c'est un début. Pour étendre la cadence et lui donner forme ayez recours aux gammes et aux arpèges – ou à la musique de Mozart. Restez simple au début et ne modulez que quand vous aurez acquis plus d'expérience. Même alors, une cadence ne devra pas comporter plus de deux modulations. Ecrivez votre cadence avec des barres de mesures. Une cadence ne doit pas être rigoureusement mesurée mais cela vous aidera à prévoir des longueurs de phrases correctes et une forme générale. Enfin, soyez patient, n'attendez pas de résultat immédiatement brillant – seul Mozart pouvait réussir cela!

Quelques exemples de cadences faciles et courtes:

1st Movement (Premier mouvement)

2nd Movement (Deuxième mouvement)

3rd Movement (Troisième mouvement)

Andante in C (*Andante* en *ut*)

1. E. and P. Badura Skoda: *Interpreting Mozart at the Keyboard* [Barry and Rockcliffe]
   Franz Vester: *On the Performance of Mozart's Flute Music* [N.F.A.]
   B.B. Mather and D. Lasocki: *The Classical WOODWIND Cadenza* [McGinnis and Marx]
   J.J. Quantz: *Versuch* [1752]
   New Grove: *Dictionary of Music and Musicians* [MacMillan]
   J. Bowers: *Mozart and the Flute* [Early Music, Feb.1993]

2. Appoggiatura: from *appoggiare* (It.) – to lean.

1. E. et P. Badura Skoda, *Interpreting Mozart at the Keyboard*, [Barry and Rockcliffe]
   Franz Vester, *On the Performance of Mozart's Flute Music*, N.F.A.
   B.B. Mather et D. Lasocki, *The Classical WOODWIND Cadenza*, [McGinnis and Marx]
   J.J. Quantz, *Versuch*, 1752
   New Grove, *Dictionary of Music and Musicians*, MacMillan
   J. Bowers, *Mozart and the Flute*, Early Music, fév.1993

2. Appoggiatura, de l'italien *Appoggiare* – pencher.

Konzert No.2 in D-dur K.314

Die beiden Flötenkonzerte, K.313 und K.314 und das Andante in C, K.315 entstanden 1778 in Mannheim aufgrund eines Auftrags des holländischen Arztes und Amateurflötisten Ferdinand Dejean (1731–1797). Dieser Auftrag, der von dem Mannheimer Hofflötisten Johann Baptist Wendling (1723–1797) bearbeitet wurde, beinhaltete 'drei kurze, einfache Konzerte und ein paar Quartette für die Flöte' gegen einen Lohn von 200 Gulden. Nachdem er das erste Konzert geschrieben hatte, stellte Mozart fest, daß ihm nicht mehr viel Zeit blieb. Um den Auftrag zu erfüllen, übertrug er sein früheres Oboenkonzert von C nach D-dur und schuf auf diese Weise das zweite Flötenkonzert.

Von den beiden Konzerten sind uns nur die folgenden Autographe überliefert: das des Andante in C und die Solooboenstimme des Oboenkonzerts; die Echtheit des letzteren wird jedoch angezweifelt. Es ist wahrscheinlich, daß das Andante in C als einfachere Variante zum zweiten Satz des D-dur Konzerts entstanden war.

Aufzeichnungen ist zu entnehmen, daß der Nachlaß eines gewissen Amateurflötisten Dejean nach seinem Tod versteigert worden war. Unter den Gegenständen befand sich auch eine Truhe mit 'Musikmanuscripten'...

Historische Instrumente Der genaue Flötentyp, der von Wendling und Dejean zur Aufführung von Mozarts Musik verwendet wurde, ist nicht bekannt. Man nimmt jedoch an, daß es sich um die einklappige Flöte handelte, die zu jener Zeit üblich war, mit vier Stücken und einem Innendurchmesser von ca.18.6 bis 19mm. Für das Konzert für Flöte und Harfe in C verwendete der Duc de Guines (ein ehemaliger Botschafter in London) jedoch sicherlich die sechsklappige englische Flöte mit ihrer Fußstückerweiterung zum tiefen C.

Mozarts 'Abneigung' gegen die Flöte Mozart schrieb am 14. Februar 1778 in einem Brief an seinen Vater über die Flöte, 'Jedes Mal, wenn ich für ein Instrument komponieren muß, das ich nicht mag, verliere ich sogleich das Interesse daran.' Mozarts Bemerkung war jedoch wahrscheinlich von der Tatsache beeinflußt, daß Dejean ihn nicht vollständig für die Konzerte und Quartette bezahlte, die er in Auftrag gegeben hatte. Es ist auch möglich, daß Mozart weniger enthusiastisch war, weil er für einen Amateurmusiker komponierte. Die Flöte mit ihren Gabelgriffen war wegen ihres unreinen Spiels bekannt, und dies veranlaßte ihn vielleicht ebenfalls zu dieser Bemerkung.

Mozarts Worte wurden häufig zitiert und übertrieben, dennoch schrieb er wundervolle Soli für die Flöte. Seine späteren Orchesterwerke zeigen keinerlei Abneigung gegen das Instrument, das er angeblich zu hassen liebte. Mozart soll darüber hinaus die folgende Beobachtung über den Flötisten Wendling gemacht haben: '...bei ihm muß man nicht immer Angst haben, daß eine Note beim Spiel viel zu hoch oder zu niedrig ist... sein Herz sitzt an der rechten Stelle, wie auch seine Ohren und seine Zungenspitze...'

Concerto N2 in Re KV.314

I due concerti per flauto, KV.313 e KV.314, e l'Andante KV.315, furono scritti a Mannheim nel 1778 su commissione di un medico olandese dilettante di flauto, Ferdinand Dejean (1731–1797). Questa commissione, il cui tramite fu il flautista di corte di Mannheim, Wendling, (Johann Baptist Wendling, 1723–1797), era per "tre semplici, brevi concerti e un paio di quartetti con il flauto, per un compenso di 200 fiorini d'oro". Dopo aver completato il primo concerto, Mozart capì che il tempo rimanente era insufficiente per adempiere al suo impegno e così trascrisse il suo precedente concerto per oboe in do maggiore nella tonalità di re maggiore, facendone il secondo concerto per flauto.

Dei due concerti le uniche parti autografe rimaste sono l'Andante in do e la parte dell'oboe solo del concerto per oboe, anche se esiste qualche dubbio sull'autenticità di quest'ultima. E probabile che l'Andante fosse stato scritto quale più facile alternativa al secondo movimento del Concerto in Re.

Si ha testimonianza che, dopo la sua morte, gli effetti di uno certo dilettante di flauto, Dejean, furono messi all'asta. Tra questi vi era un baule contenente manoscritti musicali...

Lo strumento dell'epoca L'esatto tipo di strumento usato da Wendling e Dejean per eseguire i brani di Mozart non ci è noto, ma si ritiene che fosse il flauto ad una chiave comune all'epoca, con quattro giunture e un diametro interno tra 18.6 e i 19 millimetri. Per il concerto per flauto e arpa in Do, comunque, il Duca de Guines (precedentemente ambasciatore a Londra), dovette senz'altro aver usato un flauto inglese a sei chiavi con l'estensione per il do più grave.

A Mozart non piace il flauto In una lettera a suo padre del 14 febbraio 1778, Mozart scrisse a proposito del flauto: "Ogni qualvolta che devo scrivere della musica per uno strumento che non apprezzo, il mio interesse sembra sbiadire velocemente". Questa opinione di Mozart, comunque, fu probabilmente influenzata dal fatto che Dejean non gli aveva pagato completamente il compenso per i concerti e i quartetti commissionati; ed è anche possibile che Mozart avesse meno interesse a scrivere per un dilettante. Il flauto con le sue diteggiature incrociate, si guadagnò la reputazione per essere stonato e anche questo potrebbe aver influenzato il suo atteggiamento.

La opinione di Mozart sul flauto è stata ampiamente diffusa ed esagerata, nonostante la meravigliosa musica per solo flauto che egli scrisse. Le sue composizioni successive non mostrano alcun segno di disprezzo per lo strumento che, secondo l'opinione generale, egli amava odiare. Oltre a questo Mozart fece le seguenti osservazioni su il flutista Wendling: "...non ti devi preoccupare quando sai che una nota sta per essere suonata un po' calante o un po' crescente... il suo cuore è nel posto giusto e così sono le sue orecchie e la punta della sua lingua..."

Vorgehensweise der Redaktion

Wenn nicht anders angegeben, wurden die frühsten bekannten Quellen verwandt, und die Flötenstimme kann als 'Urtext' angesehen werden. Empfohlene Feinheiten und Bindungen, die es zu Mozarts Zeit möglicherweise gab, werden durch gepunktete Linien wiedergegeben oder in Klammern gesetzt. Ausführende auf der modernen Flöte ziehen es vielleicht vor, die durchgestrichenen Bindungen wegzulassen, um längere Phrasen zu erzielen. Tuttis wurden weggelassen, obwohl der Ausführende sie, wenn er möchte, spielen kann.

Der Klavierteil ist in modernen Ausgaben in der Regel eine Verkürzung der Orchesterpartitur und deshalb häufig mit unnötigem Material vollgestopft, welches ihn – außer für die fortgeschrittensten Pianisten – unspielbar macht. Da diese Konzerte meistens mit Klavier aufgeführt werden, sind wir an das Problem des Orchesterauszugs so herangetreten, wie Mozart es getan haben mag – indem wir für das Klavier allein schrieben und nicht als Ersatz für das Orchester. Die Klavierbearbeitung nahm sich Mozarts Satz für Violin- und Klaviersonate zum Vorbild. Folglich wurde überflüssiges Material weggelassen, obwohl die ursprüngliche Notation und die Bogenführung der Streicherstimmen sorgfältig eingehalten wurden.

Aufführungsbemerkungen

Aufführungsstil Franz Vester wies darauf hin, daß diese Werke zu einer Zeit entstanden, in der der späte Barockstil in Mode war... 'es ist Tanz- und Sprechmusik – nicht Musik zum Singen'. Artikulation ist die Sprache der Musik, und Klarheit ist deshalb (zusammen mit der Verwendung von Bindungen) für diese Konzerte von besonderer Bedeutung. In der Musik des 18. Jahrhunderts sollten Bindungen auch als Diminuendo angesehen werden... mit einigen Ausnahmen! Die Bindung, und was mit ihr zusammenhängt, bestimmt somit zu einem großen Teil die Phrasierung.

Es gibt eine enge Verbindung zwischen der Solostimme und der Begleitung, und eine Untersuchung der Klavierpartitur ist wichtig, um zu sehen, inwiefern der Charakter des Orchestersatzes die Ausführung der Solostimme beeinflußen kann. Der Ausführende hat auf einer modernen Böhm-Flöte verschiedene Möglichkeiten je nach Anlaß der Aufführung; wie bereits erwähnt wurde, könnte der moderne Ausführende die durchgestrichenen Bindungen weglassen, um längere 'Linien' und Phrasen zu erhalten. Wettbewerbsteilnehmer mögen andererseits alles spielen, was Urtext ist, um negative Kritik zu vermeiden (oder sie sind klug und wählen einen Stil, den die Richter hören möchten, obwohl eine neue Interpretation auch Punkte einbringen kann). Bei einer Aufnahme muß sich der Ausführende damit abfinden, daß seine Interpretation dieses Evergreens für alle Zeit festgehalten sein wird... Flötisten unseres Jahrhunderts haben in der Regel einen romantischen Stil mit 'langlinigen' Phrasen gewählt; es ist auch üblich, lange (denkbar überlange) Kadenzen zu hören.

Linee editoriale

A parte dove altrimenti indicato, le più antiche fonti conosciute sono state seguite alla lettera e la parte del flauto può essere considerata un 'urtext'. I suggerimenti di colore e le legature probabilmente usati al tempo di Mozart sono indicati con linee punteggiate o posti tra parentesi. Gli esecutori che facciano uso del flauto moderno possono evitare le legature sbarrate con un trattino per ottenere arcate di fraseggio più ampie. I Tutti sono stati omessi, ma il solista potrà eseguirli se lo riterrà opportuno.

Le parte del piano nelle edizioni moderne è solitamente una riduzione orchestrale della partitura e di conseguenza risulta sovraccarica e di alquanto difficile esecuzione. Poichè questi concerti sono per lo più eseguiti con il pianoforte, abbiamo affrontato il problema della riduzióne orchestrale come Mozart avrebbe fatto, scrivendo una parte pianistica autonoma non una riduzióne. La parte pianistica è modellata sulla scrittura delle sonate per piano e violino. Perciò il materiale superfluo è stato omesso, nonostante la completa aderenza alla notazione originale compresi i fraseggi delle arcate degli archi.

Note per l'esecuzione

Stile dell'esecuzione Come Franz Vester ha messo in luce questi lavori sono stati scritti quando era in voga il tardo stile barocco... "questa è musica danzata e parlata, non cantata". L'articolazione è l'essènza di questa musica e perciò la nitidézza (unita all'uso della legatura) è di particolare importanza in questi concerti. Nella musica del diciottesimo secolo, la legatura era vista come un diminuendo... eccetto qualche volta! Così la legatura e ciò che ne consegue, regolano la maggior parte del fraseggio.

C'è una stretta connessione tra la parte solistica e l'accompagnamento e perciò uno studio della parte del pianoforte è importante per osservare quale influenza il carattere della scrittura orchestrale possa avere sull'esecuzione della parte solistica. Sul flauto Boehm moderno, l'esecutore ha diverse opzioni a secondo del tipo di interpretazione: come già suggerito, l'esecutore moderno, può tralasciare le legature sbarrate con un trattino per ottenere frasi e linee più lunghe. Nei concorsi per contro si può suonare tutto secondo l'originale per evitare commenti negativi (o può essere indicato suonare nello stile che i giudici desiderano acoltare, però anche approcci nuovi possono risultare vincenti). Per una registrazione, l'esecutore deve vedersela con il fatto che l'interpretazione di questo intramontabile lavoro rimarrà congelata sul disco. I Flautisti del nostro secolo hanno solitamente adottato uno stile romantico con frasi lunghe; e solitamente si ascoltano cadenze ampie, forse fin troppo.

Verzierungen CPE Bach schrieb, daß niemand jemals daran zweifelte, daß Verzierungen nötig seien. Verzierungen dienen dazu, Noten zu verbinden, um eine besondere Note oder Phrase zu beleben, und um die Aufmerksamkeit des Zuhörers auf sie zu lenken. Mozart schrieb diese Konzerte während eines Wechsels im Verzierungsstil; es ist deshalb für uns schwierig, zu wissen, wie die Verzierungen genau gespielt werden sollen. Ausführende können in dieser Ausgabe die frühesten schriftlichen Quellen sehen und dementsprechend ein Urteil abgeben. Jene, die nur wenig Spezialwissen haben, ziehen es vielleicht vor, den Vorschlägen der Redaktion zu folgen (die entweder in Klammern stehen oder über dem Liniensystem), die auf dem sachkundigen Wissen der heutigen Zeit beruhen[1]. Die beiden Verzierungen, die für uns wichtig sind, sind *Vorschläge* und *Triller*.

Vorschläge: Betonte Vorschläge erscheinen gewöhnlich als kleine Note, deren ausgeschriebener Wert nicht immer den zu spielenden Rhythmus bezeichnet. Der vorgeschlagene Rhythmus wurde über dem Liniensystem beim ersten Erscheinen angegeben; der Spieler sollte diesen in nachfolgenden Beispielen befolgen. Warum gab Mozart dann nicht einfach den zu spielenden Rhythmus an? Vorschläge[2] bezeichnen eine besondere Betonung oder eine Dissonanz; manchmal lenken sie auch die Aufmerksamkeit des Zuhörers auf die Note, bei der der Vorschlag steht. Sie sind nützliche Mittel und geben dem Ausführenden deutliche Hinweise. Es ist wichtiger, wie der Vorschlag gespielt wird, als sein genauer Wert. Er stiehlt immer die Betonung von der Note, der er zugeteilt ist und die weicher folgt. Der Vorschlag wird *immer* zur Hauptnote gebunden...und Bindung heißt *diminuendo*.
(Erster Satz)

Abbellimenti CPE Bach scrisse che nessuno mai dubitò della necessità degli abbellimenti. Essi servono a collegare note, a ravvivare note o frasi o per focalizzare l'attenzione degli ascoltatori su qualcuna di queste. Mozart scrisse questi concerti durante un periodo di transizione nello stile dell'ornamentazione per cui è difficile per noi sapere come gli abbellimenti devono essere suonati. In questa edizione, gli esecutori possono vedere le fonti scritte originali e decidere di conseguenza. I meno esperti su questo argomento potranno seguire le indicazioni editoriali (poste tra parentesi o sopra il rigo) che sono state fatte secondo i più ponderati criteri odierni[1]. Ci occuperemo qui in particolare delle appoggiature e dei trilli.

Appoggiature: le appoggiature accentate compaiono di solito come piccole note il cui valore non indica sempre il ritmo da suonare. Il ritmo suggerito è indicato sopra il rigo quando esse appaiono la prima volta; l'esecutore dovrà seguire questo anche le volte sucessive. Ma perchè Mozart non scrisse il ritmo che voleva? Le appoggiature rappresentano uno speciale accento o una dissonanza o a volte aumentano l'importanza della nota a cui si appoggiano. È un efficace strumento di fraseggio e dà una precisa indicazione all'esecutore. Il modo in cui è suonata è sempre più importante del suo esatto valore. Immancabilmente essa sottrae interesse alla nota sucessiva, che segue più leggera. L'appoggiatura e sempre legata alla nota reale... e una legatura è sempre un diminuendo.

(Primo movimento)

Zusammengesetzte Vorschläge sollten liebevoll, aber schnell gespielt werden.
(Zweiter Satz, Takte 19, 21 usw.)

Appoggiature composte devono essere eseguite disinvoltamente ma velocemente:
(Secondo movimento, battute 19, 21, ecc.)

(Dritter Satz, Takt 4)   *sollte:* deve essere eseguito:

(Terzo movimento, battuta 4)   *gespielt werden oder:* o:

Takte 60 und 61 im *Konzert für Oboe* enthalten eine alternative Tonleiterpassage. Ausführende können diese benutzen oder durch ihre eigenen in Achteln, Achteltriolen oder Sechzehnteln wirkungsvoll ersetzen. Ein Vergleich mit dem Oboenkonzert wird empfohlen.

Triller beginnen alle von oben... mit einigen Ausnahmen! Die Ausnahmen sind entweder durch Weglassung einer Nebennote gekennzeichnet oder durch die Einbeziehung der unteren Nebennote. Untere oder obere – beide werden

Le battute 60 e 61 del Concerto per Oboe, hanno un passaggio di scala ad libitum. Gli esecutori potranno farne uso o sostituirlo con uno proprio in crome (ottavi), terzine di crome o in semicrome (sedicesimi) a seconda del miglioze effetto. Si raccomanda un confronto con il *Concerto per Oboe.*

I trilli cominciano sempre dalla nota superiore, ma... con qualche eccezione! Le eccezioni sono segnalate o dall'omissione della nota ausiliaria o dall'inserimento di una nota ausiliaria inferiore.

auf dem Schlag gespielt. Der Triller beginnt auf der unteren Nebennote, wenn er von unten angegangen wird, nach einer Tonleiterpassage oder, um dem Ende eines langen Teils größere Endgültigkeit zu geben. Diese Ausgabe enthält Vorschläge bezüglich der Annäherung. Ist der Triller kurz, besonders in den schnelleren Sätzen, ist es unwichtig, ob er auf der oberen Note oder der Hauptnote beginnt.

Mozart war sich darüber im klaren, ob ein Doppelschlag am Ende eines Trillers gespielt werden sollte oder nicht. Wo nichts geschrieben steht, sollte keiner gespielt werden. Ein Doppelschlag verleiht einem Triller Endgültigkeit wie in einer Kadenz; in vielen Fällen hat der Triller jedoch nur verzierende Wirkung und soll nicht das Ende eines Teils andeuten.

(Andante in C, Takt 2) zu dem Triller:

Superiori o inferiori, le note ausiliarie devono comunque essere eseguite in battere. Il trillo inizia sulla nota inferiore quando è raggiunto da sotto, dopo un passaggio di scala, o per dare più senso di chiusura alla fine di una lunga sezione. In questa edizione si danno suggerimenti riguardo a quale soluzione scegliere. Quando il trillo è breve, specialmente nei movimenti veloci, non è importante se si inizia dalla superiore o dalla nota reale.

Mozart è chiaro riguardo a quando il trillo si conclude o meno con la risoluzione. Quando nulla è segnato, la risoluzione non deve essere eseguita. La risoluzione dà appunto un senso risolutivo al trillo, come una cadenza; in molti casi comunque il trillo è semplicemente decorativo e non è inteso per punteggiare la fine di una sezione.

(Andante in do, battuta 2) per il trillo:

passen nicht zu viele Noten. Versuchen Sie:

troppe note sarebbero fuori carattere. Si provi:

oder: o:

Kadenzen

Eine Kadenz erscheint in der Regel gegen Ende eines Satzes und bietet Gelegenheit, das Publikum zu überraschen, ihm Freude zu bereiten und es zu Beifall zu ermuntern. Die Pause auf dem Quartsextakkord wird aufgeschoben und durch Tonleitern und Arpeggien bis zum Erscheinen des Dominantseptakkords und der Auflösung unterbrochen. Entgegen der allgemeinen Auffassung waren diese Kadenzen relativ kurz, da ein Flötenspieler jeweils nur eine Note spielen konnte und deshalb die Harmonie und Melodie unterbrechen mußte, um Luft zu holen. Kadenzen wurden deshalb auf ein oder zwei Atemzüge beschränkt, um die nach vorn gerichtete Bewegung der Harmonie aufrechtzuerhalten. Der Ausführende wäre jedoch klug, wenn er für einen wichtigen Wettbewerb jene Art von Kadenz spielte, die die Jury gewöhnlich hört...
Folgendes sollte beachtet werden:
• In einer kurzen Kadenz ist es nicht nötig, das thematische Material zu zitieren.
• Versuchen Sie immer, spontan zu klingen.
• Eine Kadenz sollte ein oder zwei Überraschungen enthalten.
• Es sollte einen Höhepunkt in der Kadenz geben: manchmal ist es die höchste Note oder die schnellste Passage oder sogar die Überraschung.
• Wenn es einen kadenzierenden Triller gibt, sollte das Orchester, der Cembalist oder Pianist den Dominantseptakkord in der Mitte des Trillers spielen, um ihn bis zur Auflösung fortzusetzen. (Dieser Akkord ist in dieser Ausgabe angegeben.)

Cadenze

Una cadenza è presente generalmente verso la fine del movimento ed è una opportunità per sorprendere e deliziare il pubblico e incoraggiare gli applausi. La corona sull'accordo di quarta e sesta è sospesa e interrotta da scale e arpeggi fino alla comparsa della settima di dominante e alla sua risoluzione. Al contrario di quanto si crede queste cadenze erano relativamente brevi. Il flauto può suonare soltanto una nota per volta e ogni respiro comporta necessariamente una interruzione. Così le cadenze erano contenute in uno o due fiati per mantenere un senso di movimento nell'armonia. Per un concorso comunque il concorrente farebbe bene a eseguire il tipo di cadenza che la giuria è abituata a sentire...
Alcuni punti da tenere in mente:

• In una breve cadenza non è essenziale fare citazioni del materiale tematico.
• Sempre cercare di suonare spontanei.
• Una cadenza deve contenere una o due sorprese.
• Ci deve essere un punto culminante nelle cadenza: a volte è la nota più acuta o il passaggio più veloce o anche la sorpresa.
• Se c'è un trillo di chiusura l'orchestra o il piano o il cembalo dovrà suonare, a metà di quest'ultimo, la settima di dominante per favorire la risoluzione (l'accordo è indicato in questa edizione).

Wenn Sie Ihre eigene Kadenz unter Verwendung von Mozarts Material schreiben möchten, schauen Sie sich seine Themen an:

Per scrivere la propria cadenza sui materiali di Mozart, scorrete i suoi temi:

(Erster Satz) primo movimento

(Zweiter Satz) secondo movimento

und die verwendbare Kadenz bei 38:   e la utile cadenza al 38:

(Dritter Satz) terzo movimento

*oder die Fassung für Oboe: *o la versione per oboe:

(Andante in C) Andante in do

Suchen Sie eine kurze Phrase, um die Pause am Anfang mit dem letzten kadenzierenden Triller auf dem Dominantseptakkord zu verbinden. Zum Beispiel:
(Erster Satz)

Trovate una breve frase per collegare la corona iniziale con il trillo finale della cadenza sulla settima di dominante. Per esempio:
(primo movimento)

Eine Kadenz muß nicht auf der angegebenen Note beginnen oder auf dem abgedruckten Triller enden, oder überhaupt auf einem Triller, wobei der Wiedereintritt in das Konzert eine

La cadenza non deve necessariamente iniziare sulla nota di fermata, nè su quella del trillo stampato, nè in realta terminare con un trillo, nel qual caso il riinizio del concerto costituirebbe

CONCERTO No.2 IN D, K.314

Edited by Trevor Wye
Piano arrangement by Robert Scott

W. A. MOZART

1

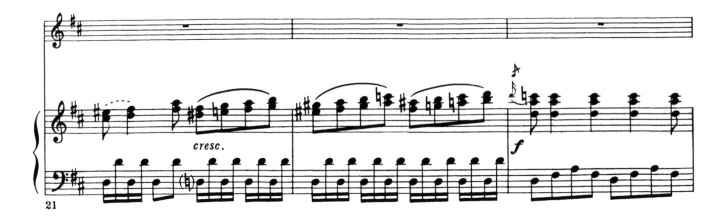

* This slur is omitted in oboe version (see Preface)

39

42

45

48

* See piano part

101

104

107

110

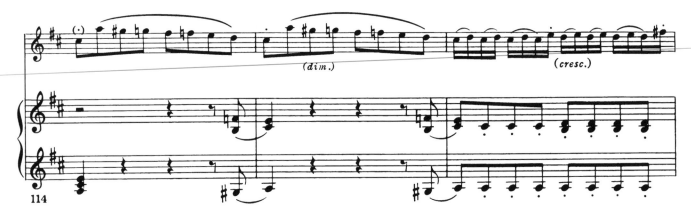

114

117

120

124

141

144

147

150

154

157

160

163

166

170

173

(See Preface)

177

2

Adagio ma non troppo

* See Preface

5

9

13

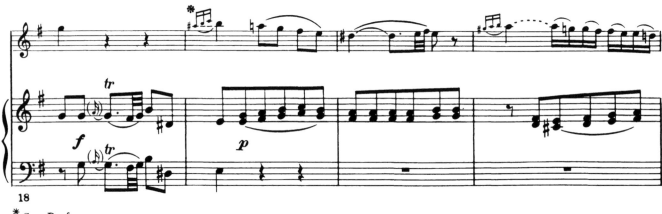

18

* See Preface

22

26

29

32

36

40

43

47

(See Preface)

3

* See Preface

13

19

25

31

* See Preface

* See Preface

24

64

70

77

83

88

93

98

103

108

114

(short cadenza)

120

126

153

159

165

170

195

201

207

213

218

224

230

235

241

246

(See Preface)

252

258

ANDANTE IN C, K.315

Edited by Trevor Wye
Piano arrangement by Robert Scott

W. A. MOZART

* See Preface

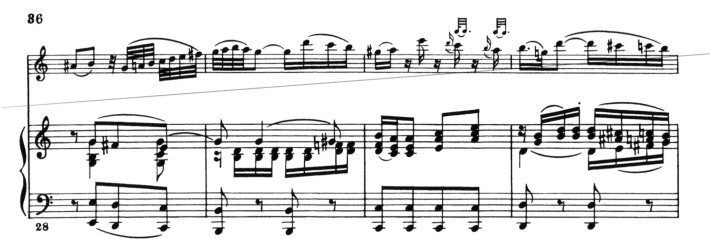

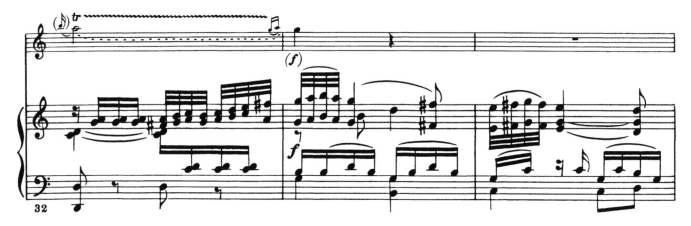

84

87

(See Preface)

91

95

Überraschung darstellen würde! In diesem Beispiel wäre ein Triller auf Cis genau so gut wie der Triller auf E:

una sorpresa! Nel seguente esempio un trillo sul do diesis è altrettanto valido di uno sul mi:

Das ist zwar noch keine Kadenz, aber ein Anfang. Um Ihre Kadenz auszudehnen, verwenden Sie Tonleitern und Arpeggien – oder Mozarts Musik – um ihr etwas Form zu verleihen. Halten Sie sie zunächst einfach und modulieren Sie erst, wenn Sie mehr Erfahrung haben; selbst dann sollte es in einer Kadenz nicht mehr als zwei Modulationen geben. Schreiben Sie Ihre Kadenz mit Taktstrichen; eine Kadenz benötigt diese nicht unbedingt, aber Sie können sie dann eher mit der korrekten Phrasenlänge und der Gesamtgestalt planen. Haben Sie schließlich Geduld; erwarten Sie kein promptes und ausgezeichnetes Ergebnis – nur Mozart konnte das!

Hier folgen einige leichte, kurze Kadenzen als Beispiele:

Questa non è ancora una cadenza, ma è un inizio. Per ampliare la cadenza, si usino scale e arpeggi – o musica di Mozart – per dargli una fisionomia. Cominciate con una cosa semplice e quando sarete più esperti potrete anche inserire qualche modulazione: ma mai più di due per ogni cadenza. Scrivete la cadenza con le linee di battuta che, anche se non strettamente necessarie, vi aiuteranno a pianifiacre la lunghezza delle frasi, e la forma generale. E infine siate pazienti: non aspettatevi risultati brillanti immediatamente – solo Mozart riusciva in questo!

Questi sono alcuni esempi di brevi cadenze come esempi:

(Erster Satz) primo movimento

(Zweiter Satz) secondo movimento

(Dritter Satz) terzo movimento

(Andante in C) Andante in do

1. E. und P. Badura-Skoda: *Interpreting Mozart at the Keyboard* [Barry and Rockcliffe]
Franz Vester: *On the Performance of Mozart's Flute Music* [N.F.A.]
B.B. Mather und D. Lasocki: *The Classical WOODWIND Cadenza* [McGinnis and Marx]
J.J. Quantz: *Versuch* [1752]
New Grove: *Dictionary of Music and Musicians* [MacMillan]
J. Bowers: *Mozart and the Flute* [Early Music, Feb.1993]

2. Appoggiatura: von *appoggiare* (It.) – unterstützen.

1. E. e P. Badura Skoda: *Interpreting Mozart at the Keyboard* [Barry and Rockcliffe]
Franz Vester: *On the Performance of Mozart's Flute Music* [N.F.A.]
B.B. Mather e D. Lasocki: *The Classical WOODWIND Cadenza* [McGinnis and Marx]
J.J. Quantz: *Versuch* [1752]
New Grove: *Dictionary of Music and Musicians* [MacMillan]
J. Bowers: *Mozart and the Flute* [Early Music, Feb.1993]

CONCERTO No.2 IN D, K.314

Edited by Trevor Wye
Piano arrangement by Robert Scott

W. A. MOZART

1

FLUTE

* This slur is omitted in oboe version (see Preface)   + See Performing Notes regarding slurs
++ See 'string' phrasing in piano part

FLUTE

+ See piano part phrasing

2

ANDANTE IN C, K.315

Edited by Trevor Wye
Piano arrangement by Robert Scott

W. A. MOZART

FLUTE

Andante

* See Preface

** There is no appoggiatura here in the autograph score

TREVOR WYE *flute* MUSIC

PRACTICE BOOKS

Invaluable to players of every grade; covering all
the technical difficulties of the instrument.

Volume 1 *Tone* (*Tone* cassette available separately)
Volume 2 *Technique*
Volume 3 *Articulation*
Volume 4 *Intonation & Vibrato*
Volume 5 *Breathing & Scales*
Volume 6 *Advanced Practice*

NOVELLO CLASSICS

A series of new editions of famous masterpieces
for the flute.

Andersen *24 Studies Op.15*
Debussy *Syrinx*
Gluck *Dance Of The Blessed Spirits*
Schubert *Theme And Variations* D.802
Bach *Suite No.2 In B minor* BWV 1067

COMPOSER ALBUMS

Interesting and enjoyable repertoire for flautists
of intermediate level.

A Couperin Flute Album
An Elgar Flute Album
A Fauré Flute Album
A Rameau Flute Album
A Ravel Flute Album
A Satie Flute Album
A Schumann Flute Album
A Vivaldi Flute Album

A First Latin-American Flute Album
A Second Latin-American Flute Album

Novello Publishing Limited